THE OPEN GATE

David Adam is the Vicar of Holy Island where his work involves ministering to thousands of pilgrims and other visitors. He was born in Alnwick, Northumberland, and worked as a coal miner before being ordained. During more than twenty years as Vicar of Danby in North Yorkshire he discovered a gift for composing prayers in the Celtic pattern. Since 1985 he has published several very popular collections of prayers and meditations based on the Celtic tradition, using material he has tried and tested with groups and individuals from his own parishes and on retreat.

D0039933

Also by David Adam

THE EDGE OF GLORY
Prayers in the Celtic Tradition 1987

THE CRY OF THE DEER
Meditations on the Hymn of St. Patrick 1988

THE OPEN GATE

Celtic Prayers

for Growing Spiritually

DAVID ADAM

---

*Illustrations by
Jean Freer*

MOREHOUSE PUBLISHING
Harrisburg, PA

First published 1994
Triangle
SPCK
First American edition
published by
Morehouse Publishing, 1995

Morehouse Publishing

Editorial Office:
871 Ethan Allen Highway
Ridgefield, CT 06877

Corporate Office:
P.O. Box 1321
Harrisburg, PA 17105

Library of Congress Cataloging-in-Publication Data

Adam, David.
    The open gate : Celtic prayers for growing spiritually / David
Adam; illustrations by Jean Freer. — 1st Amer. ed.
        p.   cm.
    Originally published: London: Triangle/SPCK, 1994.
    ISBN 0-8192-1640-2 (pbk.)
    1. Prayers.   I. Title.
BV245.A33   1995   94-44757
242' .8' 0089916—dc20   CIP

Contents

Introduction 1

PREPARATION 9

CANDLE PRAYERS 21

ADORATION 37

CONFESSION 49

INTERCESSION 59

THE OFFERING 69

THE EUCHARISTIC PRAYER 77

THANKSGIVING 85

DEDICATION 95

BLESSINGS 107

Notes 116

He has opened for us the gate of glory

Introduction

As long as we are alive, we are on the move. To become static is to stagnate and die. It is necessary for all living things to move and grow and change. Life is meant to be an adventure; change is a gift that we have to learn to use aright. In Celtic folk-tales a curse that could happen to a person was to enter a field and not to be able to get back out of it. To be stuck in that place for ever. It was seen as a definite curse to be unable to venture or to change. Yet we all know this experience in some small way; we all get ourselves stuck in routines and habits that can act like shackles. We all refuse to open our eyes to the vision that is before us; too often we select only what we want to see. In the same way we restrict what we hear and what we respond to. The open gate is the opposite to this. It is the invitation to adventure and to grow, the call to be among the living and vital elements of the world. The open gate is the call to explore new areas of yourself and the world around you. It is a challenge to come and discover that the world and ourselves are filled with mystery and with the glory of God. It is the ever present call to become pilgrims for the love of God, to take part in a romance that will enrich our hearts and our lives.

The open gate is the choice that God is always placing before us. It is a sign of the opportunity that is ours. It is to do with our basic freedom; we can choose to go that way or to ignore it and go along other paths. We should look upon the open gate as a way to extend ourselves and our vision. Here we can see further and reach beyond where we have been before. It may take a great deal of discipline to get off the old familiar track and to break with old habits, but in return it offers the excitement of new ground and new vistas. What we have to learn is to recognize when an open gate is presented to us. There are many gates, physical, mental and spiritual, through which we can travel to the 'other world', or, as I would prefer, 'to a greater vision of this world of ours'. There are always deeper levels of reality to explore. To accept open gates is to accept the role of a frontiersperson, an adventurer going where no one has gone before. Yet there are those who have made like journeys, taken similar adventures, so we are not without guides and fellow travellers. Just as when you go to a new country you can buy a guidebook to help you to get around, so in the venture of life, you can get advice and direction from those who have travelled before you. When you make this venture, you will discover riches that you never dreamed of. St Brendan of Birr says, 'If you become Christ's you will stumble upon wonder upon wonder and every one of them true.' We need to discover that Christ has opened up for us the gate of glory.

Every now and again 'our eyes are opened' and we see beyond the narrowness of our day-to-day vision. This was expressed by Jacob when he awoke out of sleep, a sleep he felt he had been in all his life up to that point: 'Jacob awoke out of sleep and said, "Surely the Lord is in this place, and I knew it not." And he was afraid, and said, "How aweful is this place! This is none other than the house of God, and this is the gate of heaven"' (Genesis 28.16–17). Jacob had not been looking for this experience, it had suddenly opened before him. I believe that such experiences are offered to all of us at one time or another in our lives. But we in our turn have to be open enough to receive them. Such new vistas often come before us at a point of crisis in our lives, when we are suddenly bereaved, or made redundant, or when we are having what the world calls a breakdown. Often we become more aware because we have become dislocated, just as we are more aware of a limb that is dislocated. If we face the unfamiliar it may open all sorts of gates for us.

Prayer is not an escape from such situations but an entering deeper into the reality of what is going on around us. Prayer should help us to extend ourselves and our lives. Prayer will not rescue us from the situation, but it should help us to see it more clearly, and to recognize that we are not alone in it. However, we cannot stop the greater reality breaking in upon us if we want to go on living life fully. Life is forever presenting us with new openings and with all the mysteries of our universe.

> Just when we are safest, there's a sunset-touch,
> A fancy from a flower-bell, some one's death,
> A chorus ending from Euripides,
> And that's enough for fifty hopes and fears
> As old and new at once as nature's self
> To rap and knock and enter into our soul.
>
> *Robert Browning*[1]

This gate will open to us in quite an unexpected way and show us a world we never dreamed was there, and yet it was with us all the time. It is not that a new world is born, rather that we have awakened out of sleep to behold the gate of glory. This is expressed well by Wordsworth in his poem 'Tintern Abbey':

> And I have felt
> A presence that disturbs me with the joy
> Of elevated thoughts; a sense sublime
> Of something far more deeply interfused,
> Whose dwelling is the light of setting suns,
> And the round ocean and the living air,
> And the blue sky, and in the mind of man . . .

Wordsworth did not create this 'presence', he became

aware of it and responded to it. He does it again in his poem 'Intimations of Immortality':

> To me the meanest flower that blows can give
> Thoughts that do often lie too deep for tears.

At other times the gate will only open if we work at it. Out in the open country there are few gates that open automatically, and there are many that take a great deal of effort to get open. If we seek to loose the latch or make an effort to find the key, there are many gates that open on to secret gardens. If we are lucky, we may stumble upon one of them.

> . . . suddenly the gust of wind swung aside some loose ivy trails, and more suddenly still she jumped towards it and caught it in her hand. This she did because she had seen something under it – a round knob which had been covered by the leaves hanging over it. It was the knob of a door . . . Mary's heart began to thump and her hands to shake a little in her delight and excitement . . . What was this under her hands which was square and made of iron and which her fingers found a hole in? . . . it was the lock of the door which had been closed ten years, and she put her hand in her pocket, drew out the key, and found it fitted the keyhole. She put the key in and turned it. It took two hands to do it, but it did turn . . . then she slipped through it, and shut it behind her, and stood with her back against it, looking about her and breathing quite fast with excitement, and wonder, and delight.
> She was standing *inside* the secret garden.[2]

There are times when we must seize the opportunity when it is offered to us. Some things happen only once and if we miss the chance, we may not have it again. In the parable of the wise and foolish virgins there comes a time when the door is shut and those who ought to have been able to share in the celebration find the way closed to them; the opportunity has passed and they have missed out. Yet, to balance this, our God gives us many opportunities to know Him. St John the Divine says of heaven in the book of Revelation, 'and the gates thereof shall in no wise be shut' (Revelation 21.25). The gates are open for wanderers, latecomers, penitents, and anyone who seeks to come that way.

We give thanks that our Lord has 'opened for us the gate of glory', though we need to make the effort to go through. We are given an invitation but we will not be forced to enter. If we are to enter, we must move towards the gate; we may have to find out where the gate is, and how to approach it. For different people the approach may be from different angles: some will learn to 'come into His gates with thanksgiving', others will need to come through penitence and forgiveness. There are those who will come through quiet adoration and others through personal dedication. All of us will learn to use each of these gates at one time or another. In the Communion service all the various gates are offered to us and there are many invitations to come and enter in common union with Him.

Through this book we shall look at such invitations and use them to become more aware that the kingdom of heaven is at hand. We may even learn with Julian of Norwich that we are more in heaven than on earth. We can discover with the woman from Kerry in Ireland that 'heaven is just one foot six inches above us' and if we but stretch ourselves we can touch it if not enter into it. We must learn to extend our vision, to be more alert in our hearing, to be sensitive in our dealings, and open-hearted. It is then that new vistas will be more able to present themselves to us. In it all, it is not that we make God come, He is with us already. The gate of glory is already open and He is inviting us to enter into it. He is with us and calling us to adventure with Him.

The layout of the book follows the traditional pattern of the Communion service and is meant to be of use to those new to the church: people who have recently come, or come back to, Christian commitment, or who have just been confirmed. But it can just as easily be used by those who are seeking to learn prayer, or seeking to renew a prayer life that has somehow become too fixed. It will begin with prayers of preparation, a time to centre ourselves on His presence and His love. All prayer needs to start here, affirming that we are in His presence and that He is with us wherever we are. We forever need to be reminding ourselves, 'The Lord is here. His Spirit is with us'. The candle prayers that follow this are still about placing ourselves in His presence and acknowledging His power and His love. These prayers can be used at the candle lighting in a church, though I hope they will also be used at home. I have offered at this point a little service that can be used morning and evening at home or with friends.

Once we realize the presence we cannot help but adore. There needs to be a time when we give our love to God as He has given His love to us. We need to respond to all that He has done and is doing for us. Knowing His love brings out this response, and it also makes us realize our unworthiness. The realization that 'He who made the heavens and the earth' is willing to give Himself to us cannot but be humbling. We also realize that in His loving presence, 'all hearts are open and no secrets are hidden'. Adoration and Confession often come together as reactions to the love of God.

The most classic example of this is the call of the prophet Isaiah. Isaiah is aware of the worship of heaven declaring, 'Holy, holy, holy, The Lord Almighty is Holy! His glory fills the world', and his response is, 'There is no hope for me! I am doomed because every word that passes my lips is sinful,' (Isaiah 6.1–8). Against the love and glory of God we all become aware of our own inadequacies and sinfulness, but also of the love and forgiveness of God.

This love and forgiveness is something that we cannot keep to ourselves, we need to share it, to let it radiate out from us. The best way to receive God's gifts is to seek to give them away. If we pour love out, God pours it in; if we give peace, God gives peace to us. But if we seek these things only for ourselves they are in danger of stagnating and dying. Gifts of love, joy and peace, like talents, atrophy if they are not used. We reach out in love to our neighbours through intercession, knowing that God loves and cares for them. We come to Him knowing that He alone can make us whole. We come also in thanksgiving for all that He has done for us. All of this is acted out in the great drama of the Eucharist, where we show that we dwell in Him and He in us.

As He has given us life and love, we seek to respond. He has given us more than these precious gifts. He gives us Himself, so we seek to respond by dedicating ourselves to Him, and to the world which He loves. Not only do we give ourselves to God, we seek to give ourselves for the world, sharing in that great love with which He so loved the world that He gave Himself for it. Throughout all this our God is with us giving us new opportunities and pouring upon us His blessing. The blessings are almost coming back to where we started for they are to do with the reality of the presence. Wherever He is – and there is no place where He is not – His gifts are always being showered upon us. We are asked to respond, to go through the gate of glory and discover that we dwell in Him and He in us. I invite you to come share this adventure, to discover the joy and newness of each day, and the riches that our God offers to us. He has opened the gate of glory and invites us to enter there this very day.

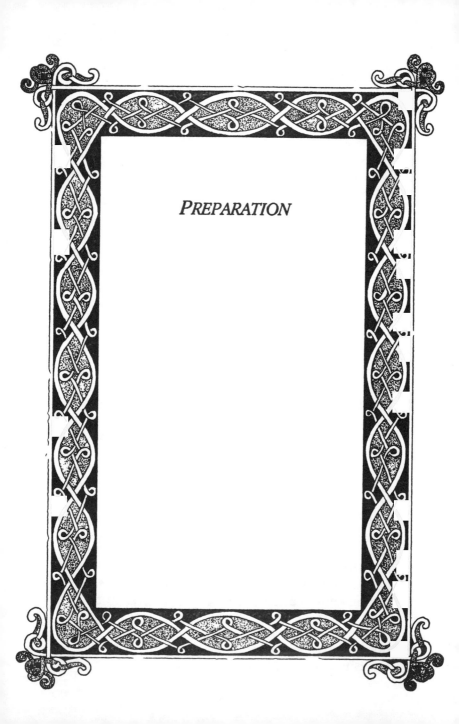

PREPARATION

We all need to prepare ourselves for prayer, just as we get ourselves ready for meeting a friend. There are things we will want to share, and events we will want to talk about. We may want a bit of support or guidance, we may want to offer to do some work for our friend. We may come full of fears and anxieties, or full of joy and love. Very often it is a mixture of all these things; our friends and our God will accept us as we are and who we are. Yet we will be able to share more and receive more if we are relaxed. One of the best preparations for prayer is relaxation. We need to learn to be still in body, mind and spirit, to let go of the tensions of our lives. We need to heed the words 'Be still and know that I am God.' It is only by relaxing into His presence that we make room for God to work, make room for His peace, His love, His joy to flow into us and through us to others.

So often nothing happens in our prayers because we do not expect anything to happen. In fact, we do not allow anything to happen; we crowd out the very gifts and the presence that we say we desire. Too often we come unprepared, cluttered, too full of all sorts. We may as well put up the notice which says 'No room at the inn'. The saying is still true: 'He came unto His own and His own received Him not.' We must learn to make time and to make room, to make space to allow our God to work. At home we should make much of silence, create little moments when we affirm God's presence, when we declare that our God is with us. We need to have times when we open ourselves and our lives to God. Just as we give our friends time and attention we need to do the same with God. Learn to pause in God's presence with such statements as 'The Lord is here'; seek to know that it is not a request but a reality that we have to become sensitive and open to. God's presence is a fact and we have to peel away all that stops us from becoming unaware of Him. We have to give Him time to refresh, renew and restore us.

The best preparation for church worship is regular daily worship at home. The words in church can only have depth and meaning if we use them at home. Too often church worship is weak because we have not been faithful in our own daily prayers. It is like trying to be friendly on a Sunday to someone you have ignored all week. At least remember, if you have forgotten God, He has not forgotten you. If you hardly know Him, He knows you. Even if you are unaware of Him, He is well aware of you.

To use John Donne's words, we need to 'tune the instrument here at the door', to prepare ourselves for entrance into the fullness of worship. It is a good habit to make sure you bring with you the things you need: some space and openness to let God enter. If you are already occupied with other things, awareness of His coming will be weakened. Come with the desire to adore, seek to give your love to Him as He gives His love to you. No doubt there will be something you want to confess, something that you know has let Him and yourself down. Bring it and admit it and know His forgiving love. Learn to enter His gates with thanksgiving; it is one of the easiest ways into God's presence. Pray for yourself, for others and for the world to which you belong, knowing that God is willing and able to answer our prayers. If you come with nothing, expecting nothing, you should not be surprised if you go away with nothing. Though God is good, often He will invade our nothingness and create something of His glory.

Know also that God cannot be boring; it is only our own preoccupation and fullness that bores us. If the service is full of phrases like 'The Lord is with you', or 'With angels and archangels' it cannot be dull; it must be you who have become dull, or at least out of tune. Prepare for worship, tune the instrument at the gate, and you and your worship will be enriched.

In the mighty name of God,
In the saving name of Jesus,
In the strong name of the Spirit,
We come
We cry
We watch
We wait
We look
We long
For you.

In the love of the Father,
In the light of Christ,
In the leading of the Spirit,
We place ourselves today.

In the praise of the Creator,
In the presence of the Saviour,
In the power of the Spirit,
We come.

The Lord be with you
And also with you
Father be with us
Amen
The Creator be with you
And also with you
Christ be with us
Amen
The Saviour be with you
And also with you
Spirit be with us
Amen
The Strengthener be with you
And also with you
Trinity be with us
Amen
The Holy Three be with you
And also with you
God be with us
Amen

The Lord is here
His Spirit is with us

We need not fear
His Spirit is with us.

We abide in peace
His Spirit is with us

We are immersed in love
His Spirit is with us

We continue in hope
His Spirit is with us

We rejoice in faith
His Spirit is with us.

Lord, help us to know that you are here and with us now,
That your Spirit is with us and abides with us always.

Lord, open our eyes
And we shall behold your glory.

Lord, open our ears
And we shall hear your call.

Lord, open our hearts
And we shall know your love.

Lord, open our hands
And we shall show your generosity.

Lord, open our lives
And we shall reveal your glory.

You, Lord, are in this place
Your presence fills it
Your presence is Peace.

You, Lord, are in my heart
Your presence fills it
Your presence is Peace.

You, Lord, are in my mind
Your presence fills it
Your presence is Peace.

You, Lord, are in my life
Your presence fills it
Your presence is Peace

Help us, O Lord, to know that we dwell in you
and you dwell in us this day and for evermore.

Awaken me to your presence,
Alert me to your love,
Affirm me in your peace.
Open to me your way,
Reveal to me your joy,
Enfold me in your light.
For my heart is ready,
Lord, my heart is ready.

Lord, help me to relax.

Take from me the tension
that makes peace impossible.
Take from me the fears
that do not allow me to venture.
Take from me the worries
that blind my sight.
Take from me the distress
that hides your joy.

Help me to know
that I am with you,
that I am in your care,
that I am in your love,
that you and I are one.

In you we live and move.
In you we have our being.
We are in your love
Enfolded in your peace
Surrounded by your might.

Open our eyes, Lord,
Enlarge our vision.
Open our hearts, Lord,
Increase our faith.
Open our minds, Lord,
Deepen our knowing.

We are in your love
Enfolded in your peace
Surrounded by your might.
In you we live and move.
In you we have our being.

The Lord is with us,
With might to protect us,
With strength to defend us.
The Lord is with us.

The Lord is with us,
With wisdom to guide us,
With peace to refresh us.
The Lord is with us.

The Lord is with us,
With love to enfold us,
With joy to crown us.
The Lord is with us.

The Lord is with us
This day and this night,
Now and for ever.
The Lord is with us.

Where I wander – You!
Where I ponder – You again, always You!
You! You! You!
When I am gladdened – You!
When I am saddened – You!
Only You. You again, always You!
You! You! You!
You above! You below!
In every trend, at every end.
Only You. You again, always You!
You! You! You!

Levi Yitzchak of Beritchev[1]

Cleanse the thoughts of our hearts
by the inspiration of your Holy Spirit,
that we may perfectly love you,
and worthily magnify your holy name;
through Christ our Lord. Amen.

ASB[2]

CANDLE PRAYERS

These prayers are for the beginning and the ending of the day. It may help you to light a candle as a symbol of the presence and the power of God to triumph over every darkness. It is good to look at the flame and thank God that His light conquers the darkness, to affirm that no matter how dark it gets, the darkness cannot put this light out. Remember also the proverb which says, 'It is better to light one candle than to complain about the darkness.' These are prayers that can be used whilst the candles are being lit in church as well as in your own home.

The Celtic church had a great love for light as a symbol. St Patrick lit the fire at Tara to show that the light of Christ had conquered the darkness and triumphed over death. The druids rightly warned the king that if he did not have this fire extinguished it would burn for ever in Ireland. At St Brigid's monastery the flame was never allowed to go out and it is said that the fire burned there for over a thousand years, a sign that 'Christ is the Light of the World. A Light that no darkness can quench.'

The pattern I suggest for a short morning or evening act of worship is drawn from *The Promise of His Glory*[1] and commended for use in the Church of England by the House of Bishops. It is good to begin in the dark, with a lighted taper or lighter and say:

> The Lord is my light and my salvation.
> *The Lord is my light and my salvation.*
> The Lord is the strength of my life.
> *The Lord is my light and my salvation.*
> Glory be to the Father, and to the Son, and to the
>   Holy Spirit.
> *The Lord is my Light and my salvation.*

This is followed by a short reading of Scripture. If you want a fixed reading use John 1.1–5:

> In the beginning was the Word,
> and the Word was with God, and the Word was
>   God.
> He was with God in the beginning;
> all things were made through him,
> and without him was not anything made that was
>   made.
> In him was life, and the life was the light of men.
> The light shines in the darkness,
> and the darkness has not overcome it.

Alternatively, you could read Colossians 1.12–13:

> Give thanks to the Father,
> who has delivered us from the dominion of
>   darkness
> and made us partakers in the inheritance of the
>   saints in light.

Then light the candle and say:

> Jesus Christ is the Light of the world:
> *a light no darkness can quench.*

Here you could add the words of a hymn about light if you would like to. Then comes one of the candle prayers. I have tried to have a pattern with the candle prayers so we give thanks each day for something different: Sunday is the resurrection; Monday is creation; Tuesday is world affairs; Wednesday is mission; Thursday is peace; Friday is salvation; Saturday is the saints in glory.

There are plenty of other candle prayers for you to devise a pattern of your own. After the candle prayer, it is good to have a short time of intercession and affirmation, then to end your act of worship by remembering God's blessing upon all of us.

Sunday – Resurrection

Come, Lord, in the dawning,
Come in the newness of the morning,
Come, make yourself known at the break of day
and in the breaking of the bread.

Risen Lord, come stand among us,
Awaken us to your presence,
Open to us the gate of glory,
Show us the path of life,
Help us to know you are with us now and always.

Monday – Creation

Blessed are you,
Lord God of all creation.
You have called us out of darkness into light.
Open our eyes to your presence,
Open our ears to your call,
Open our hearts to your love,
Father, Son, and Holy Spirit.

Blessed are you, Lord God,
Creator and preserver of all.
Maker of all, may we work for you,
Lover of all, may we love with you,
Giver of all, may we give like you,
Father, Son, and Holy Spirit.

Tuesday – World affairs

———

Blessed are you, Lord God, the Maker of all things.
You have brought all things into being;
You give us light,
You give us love,
You give us yourself.
Help us to give ourselves to you,
Father, Son, and Holy Spirit.

Blessed are you, Lord God, Creator of all peoples,
Giver of life and health and love.
Help us to see you in the world's needs,
To see your presence in the poor,
To serve you in serving others,
Father, Son, and Holy Spirit.

Wednesday – Mission

Blessed are you, Lord God, Creator of all.
You have called us out of darkness
Into your bright light,
Into Christ's light.
Let his presence guide us this day,
That we may share his light
And walk before you as children of light,
Father, Son, and Holy Spirit.

Creator of light,
The blessing of light be upon us –
The blessing of daylight,
The blessing of sunlight,
The blessing of Christ light.
Scatter the darkness from before us
That we may walk as children of light.

Thursday – Peace

Blessed are you, Creator and giver of peace.
Peace be upon us,
Peace be upon this place,
Peace be upon this day.
The deep, deep peace of God which the world
    cannot give,
Be upon us and remain with us always.

Blessed are you, sovereign Lord of all.
From you comes peace;
Open our lives to your peace,
Open our dealings to your peace,
Fill our world with your peace,
That we may live together in peace,
And worship you, Father, Son, and Holy Spirit.

Friday – Salvation

Blessed are you, Father, Son, and Holy Spirit.
You made the world in your love,
You redeemed the world by your love,
You sustain the world with your love.
May we ever abide in your love,
And give ourselves to you in love,
Father, Son, and Holy Spirit.

Blessed are you, Lord God of our salvation.
You have rescued us from darkness,
You have released us from fear,
You have redeemed us from death,
You have made us your children.
We worship you, Father, Son, and Holy Spirit.

Saturday – The Saints in Glory

Good and gracious God,
Grant us a glimpse of your glory.
Deliver us from the darkness of night,
Give us a share with your saints in light,
That we may live to your glory,
Father, Son, and Holy Spirit.

Blessed are you, Lord of light and love,
You have surrounded us by so great a cloud of
    witnesses.
Let us lay aside the sin that so easily besets us,
And run with patience the race that is set before us,
Looking to Jesus, the author and finisher of our faith.

Blessed are you, Lord, surrounded by the saints
    in glory.
Grant us the light of love which never fails,
That it may burn in us and shed its light around us,
Until we come to you, and your saints in
    everlasting light,
Father, Son, and Holy Spirit.

Extra candle prayers

Christ light be with us in the morning,
Christ light be with us at the end,
Christ light be with us in the dawning,
Christ light everlasting friend.

Light of God to give us hope
Power of God to protect us
Light of God to give us joy
Peace of God to calm us
Light of God to give us faith
Grace of God to save us
 This night and evermore.

My dearest Lord,
Be thou a bright flame before me
Be thou a guiding star above me
Be thou a smooth path beneath me
Be thou a kindly shepherd behind me
Today and for evermore.

St Columba (521–597)

Eternal light, shine in our hearts.
Eternal goodness, deliver us from evil.
Eternal power, be our support.
Eternal wisdom, scatter the darkness of our
    ignorance.
Eternal pity, have mercy upon us;
that with all our heart and mind and strength
we may seek thy face and be brought by thine
    infinite mercy
to thy holy presence, through Jesus Christ our Lord.
    Amen

Alcuin (735–804)

O Lord Jesus Christ, who art the very bright sun of
the world, ever rising and never going down: shine,
we beseech thee, upon our spirit, that the night of sin
and error being driven away by thy inward light, we
may walk without stumbling as in the day.
Grant this, O Lord, who livest and reignest with the
Father and the Holy Ghost for evermore. Amen.

Prymer (1559)[2]

God, kindle Thou in my heart within
A flame of love to my neighbour,
To my foe, to my friend, to my kindred all,
To the brave, to the knave, to the thrall,
O Son of the loveliest Mary,
From the lowliest thing that liveth,
To the Name that is highest of all.

Carmina Gadelica[3]

Stir our hearts on fire with love to thee, O Christ
   our God,
that in its flame we may love thee with all our heart,
with all our mind, with all our soul and with all
   our strength,
and our neighbours as ourselves,
so that keeping thy commandments,
we may glorify thee, the giver of all good gifts.

Eastern Orthodox Kontakion[4]

O thou who camest from above,
The pure celestial fire to impart,
Kindle a flame of sacred love
On the mean altar of my heart.

There let it for thy glory burn
With inextinguishable blaze,
And trembling to its source return
In humble prayer and fervent praise.

Charles Wesley (1707–1788)

O Christ my light
O Christ my shield.
O Christ my light
O Christ my protector.
O Christ my light
O Christ my strong tower.
O Christ my light
O Christ my encircler.
Guard me in your night,
Keep me in your light,
Each day, each night,
Now and for evermore,
Now and for evermore.

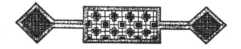

Alleluia! Christ is risen.
He is risen indeed. Alleluia!
ASB

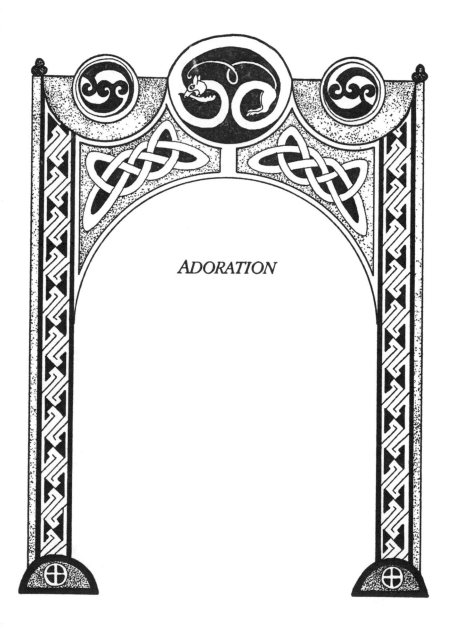

ADORATION

The great commandment is about love: 'You shall love the Lord your God, with all your heart, with all your soul, with all your mind, and with all your strength.' We are invited to give ourselves to the God who gives himself to us. As He loves us, we are invited to love Him. What God asks from us in return for all that He gives us is a response of reciprocal love. It is in loving Him that we discover how He first loved us, and how deep His love is. This is not so much a law but an invitation to us, and a delight. If we cannot enjoy time in His presence we have hardly begun to love. If we do not put ourselves out to share with Him, we can hardly say we love Him. Yet once again, even if we do not love Him, He loves us with an everlasting love. I like the words of Teilhard de Chardin concerning adoration: 'To adore means to lose oneself in the unfathomable, to plunge into the inexhaustible, to find peace in the incorruptible, to be absorbed in defined immensity, to offer oneself to the fire . . . and to give of one's deepest to that whose depth has no end.'[1] At its simplest and deepest it was expressed by a peasant woman before the altar who said, 'I look at Him and He looks at me.'

We need to learn that God made us for His love and from His love. Along with Augustine we can say, 'Lord you made us for yourself and our hearts are restless until they rest in you.' God made our hearts, our lives, to have a capacity for the eternal, and nothing less can fill them to satisfaction. It is essential that our heart is involved in all our attempts at worship. There is good advice from *Hebridean Altars*: 'The King is knocking. If thou would'st have thy share of heaven on earth, lift the latch and let in the King . . . I wait with love's expectancy. Lord Jesus, trouble not to knock at my door. My door is always on the latch. Come in, dear guest and be my host and tell me all Thy mind.'[2]

Father, you give us life,
Jesus, you give us love,
Spirit, you give wisdom,
Holy Three, you give us yourself.
Help us, O Holy One,
To give our lives
To give our love
To give our minds
To give ourselves
To you.

The love of the Creator fill my heart,
The love of the Saviour fill my heart,
The love of the Sanctifier fill my heart.
The love of the Three fill my heart,
The love of the One fill my heart.
Let that love abide and never depart.
Let that love abide and never depart.

I give myself to you, Lord,
I give myself to you.
I give my hopes to you, Lord,
I give my hopes to you.
I give my love to you, Lord,
I give my love to you.
I give my fears to you, Lord,
I give my fears to you.
Let your love set me free, Lord,
Let your love set me free.
Give yourself to me, Lord,
Give yourself to me.
Let me abide in you, Lord,
Let me abide in you,
As you abide in me, Lord,
As you abide in me.

I am bending my knee
In the eye of the Father who created me,
In the eye of the Son who purchased me,
In the eye of the Spirit who cleansed me,
    In friendship and affection.
Through Thine own Anointed One, O God,
Bestow upon us fullness in our need,
        Love towards God,
        The affection of God,
        The smile of God,
        The wisdom of God,
        The grace of God,
        The fear of God,
        And the will of God
To do on the world of the Three,
As angels and saints
Do in heaven;
    Each shade and light
    Each day and night,
    Each time in kindness,
    Give Thou us Thy Spirit.

Carmina Gadelica[3]

Thanks be to Thee, Jesu Christ,
  For the many gifts Thou hast bestowed on me,
Each day and night, each sea and land,
  Each weather fair, each calm, each wild.

I am giving Thee worship with my whole life,
  I am giving Thee assent with my whole power,
I am giving Thee praise with my whole tongue,
  I am giving Thee honour with my whole utterance.

I am giving Thee reverence with my whole
  understanding,
  I am giving Thee offering with my whole thought,
I am giving Thee praise with my whole fervour,
  I am giving Thee humility in the blood of the Lamb.

I am giving Thee love with my whole devotion,
  I am giving Thee kneeling with my whole desire,
I am giving Thee love with my whole heart,
  I am giving Thee affection with my whole sense,
I am giving Thee my existence with my whole mind,
  I am giving Thee my soul, O God of all gods.

Carmina Gadelica[4]

Glorificamus Te!
I offer Thee
Every flower that ever grew
Every bird that ever flew
Every wind that ever blew
                    Good God!
Every thunder rolling
Every church bell tolling
Every leaf and sod
                    Laudamus Te!
I offer Thee
Every wave that ever moved
Every heart that ever loved
Thee, thy Father's Well-beloved
                    Dear Lord!
Every river dashing
Every lightning flashing
Like an angel's sword
                    Benedicimus Te!
I offer Thee
Every cloud that ever swept
O'er the skies, and broke and wept
In rain, and with the flowerlets slept
                    My King!
Every communicant praying
Every angel staying
Before Thy throne to sing
                    Adoramus Te!

I offer Thee
Every flake of virgin snow,
Every spring of earth below
Every human joy and woe,

My love!
O Lord! And all thy glorious
Self o'er death victorious
Throned in heaven above

Glorificamus Te!

Ancient Irish Prayer

You are holy, Lord, the only God,
You do wonders.

You are strong, you are great,
You are the most high.
You are the almighty King.
Holy, Holy Father, the King of heaven and earth.

You are Three and One, Lord God of gods;
You are good, all good, the highest good,
Lord, God, living and true.

You are love, charity.
You are wisdom;
You are humility;
You are patience;
You are beauty;
You are meekness;
You are security;
You are inner peace;
You are joy;
You are our hope and joy;
You are justice;
You are moderation;
You are all our riches;
You are enough for us.

You are beauty, you are meekness;
You are the protector,
You are our guardian and defender;
You are strength, you are refreshment.

You are our hope, you are our faith,
You are our charity,
You are all our sweetness,
You are our eternal life:
Great and wonderful Lord,
God almighty, Merciful Saviour.

St Francis of Assisi (1181–1226)[6]

Glorious Lord, I give you greeting!
Let the church and the chancel praise you,
Let the chancel and the church praise you,
Let the plain and the hillside praise you . . .
Let the dark and the daylight praise you.
Abraham, founder of the faith, praise you.
Let the life everlasting praise you,
Let the birds and honeybees praise you . . .
Let the male and the female praise you,
Let the seven days and the stars praise you,
Let the air and the ether praise you,
Let books and letters praise you,
Let the fish in the swift streams praise you,
Let the thought and the action praise you,
Let the sand grains and the earth clods praise you.
And I shall praise you, Lord of Glory:
Glorious God, I give you greeting.

from *The Earliest Welsh Poetry*[5]

Blessing and honour, thanksgiving and praise
more than we can utter,
more than we can conceive,
be unto Thee, O holy and glorious Trinity,
Father, Son, and Holy Spirit,
by all angels, all men, all creatures,
for ever and ever.

Lancelot Andrewes (1555–1626)

Glory to God in the highest,
and peace to his people on earth . . .
we worship you, we give you thanks,
we praise you for your glory.

ASB

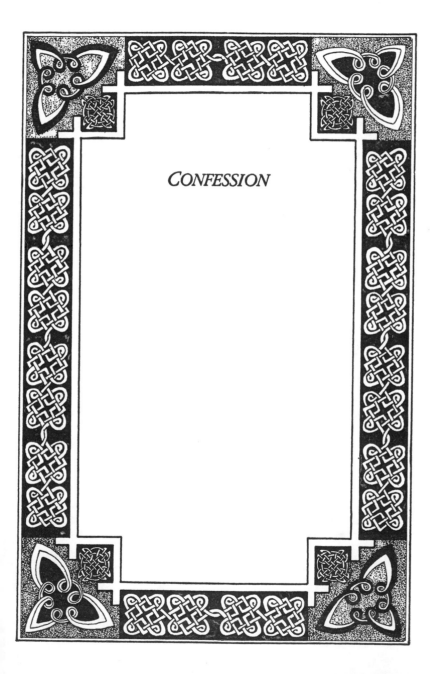

CONFESSION

Anyone who faces life realistically will be aware of their own failure, the inability to live up to their own ideals; they will be aware that they are often living well under par. We all have memories that we are ashamed of. Often the nearer we come to the brightness of the Presence the more our passions and actions reveal their darkness and shadow. We must face the truth of who we are, and know that God still loves us. God certainly does not like the sin, but He does love the sinner. He will not let us go because we have let go of Him. If we will allow Him, He will refresh and restore, He will forgive us. Here is an approach from Evelyn Underhill:

> Say to our Lord, 'Penetrate these deep murky corners where we hide memories, and tendencies on which we do not care to look, but which we will not disinter, and yield freely to you, then you may purify and transmute them. The persistent buried grudge, the half acknowledged enmity which is still smouldering; the bitterness of that loss we have not turned into sacrifice, the private comforts we cling to, the secret fears of failure which saps our initiative and is really inverted pride; the pessimism which is an insult to your joy. Lord, we bring these to you, and we review them with shame and penitence in your steadfast light.'[1]

If confession is to be real it must be an acknowledgement of our openness to, and our desire for change. Confession is often the discovery that the gate is open. If we turn like the Prodigal Son and say, 'Father, I have sinned before heaven and before you', we will discover that not only has the Father come to meet us in our turning but He welcomes us with open arms. We have it on no less authority than our Lord that 'there is more joy in heaven over one sinner that repents than over ninety-nine just persons that need no repentance.'

We also need to realize that it is only the living that are tempted! The more alive we are to life, the more we are open to temptation. The higher we are able to climb, the further we can fall. The more sensitive we are, the more open and loving, the more we will be tempted into all sorts of errors. But let it be said, it is better in life to have tried and failed than never to have tried at all. God is good, He knows our weakness, He loves us and is ready to forgive.

Often what we must learn to do is forgive, as God forgives us. Probably for many of us the hardest person to forgive is ourselves. We must learn of that deep love that God has for us; He accepts us for who we are and so gives us the power to become who we ought to be. (Note, He accepts us *before* we have changed.) We also need to learn to forgive others, or we should not pray, 'Forgive us our sins, as we forgive those who sin against us'. Often we can only receive forgiveness if we are willing to forgive. Like so many of God's gifts, forgiveness is given to us that we may be able to give it to others. Forgiveness is an attitude of God towards us and He asks us to reflect it in our attitude towards others.

We come to you, Lord, for you alone can heal
　　and restore us.
We are not able to heal ourselves,
We are not able to forgive ourselves,
We are not able to restore ourselves,
We are not able to sanctify ourselves,
We are not able to satisfy ourselves.
We come to you, Lord, for you alone can make
　　us whole.

Lord, we have fallen into sin,
We have fallen into wickedness,
We have fallen into evil.
　　　Lord, lift us up and set us free.
Lord we have fallen into rebellion,
We have fallen into disobedience,
We have fallen into unrighteousness.
　　　Lord, lift us up and set us free.
Lord we have fallen into despair,
We have fallen into disillusionment,
We have fallen into depression.
　　　Lord, lift us up and set us free.
Lord we have fallen into loneliness,
We have fallen into darkness,
We have fallen into hell.
　　　Lord, lift us up and set us free.

52

Lord of light, enter our past,
Dispel the works of darkness,
Destroy the deeds of evil,
Defeat the thoughts of blackness.
Enter the recording room of our memories,
Enter the dark room of guilt and shame,
Enter the secret room of sins hidden or forgotten.
Come, Lord of Light, and forgive.
Come, Lord of Love, and set us free.
Come, and scatter our darkness.
Come, draw us closer to you.

For the dullness of our vision,
Father forgive.
For the weakness of our faith,
Jesus forgive.
For the joylessness of our living,
Spirit forgive.
Holy Three have mercy upon us,
Forgive us our sins,
Help us to seek,
Help us to see,
Help us to serve you.

Holy and strong One
Forgive our weakness.
Holy and wise One
Forgive our foolishness.
Holy and loving One
Forgive our hardness.
Holy and generous One
Forgive our selfishness.
Holy and faithful One
Forgive our fickleness.
Holy'and gentle One
Forgive our toughness.
Forgive us, Holy One,
Forgive.

Lord, we heard that you were hungry
And we did not share our food.
Forgive us, Lord, forgive.

Lord, we heard that you were thirsty
And we kept our drink to ourselves.
Forgive us, Lord, forgive.

Lord, we saw you as a stranger
And we closed our door and our heart.
Forgive us, Lord, forgive.

Lord, we saw you go naked
And we fussed about our clothes.
Forgive us, Lord, forgive.

Lord, we discovered that you were sick
And we avoided contact with you.
Forgive us, Lord, forgive.

Lord, we heard that you were in prison
And we pretended we did not know you.
Forgive us, Lord, forgive.

Lord, you came to us again and again
And we were closed up in ourselves.
Forgive us, Lord, forgive.

To you, Lord, all hearts are open.
Forgive our secret sins
Forgive our habitual sins
Forgive our unnoticed sins;
Our sins of thought,
Word,
and deed,
All that we have left undone;
Our sins against ourselves,
Our sins against others,
Our sins against you,
All where we have fallen short of your Glory
And not done what you have called us to do.

Jesus Christ, Son of God, Saviour, have mercy
on me a sinner.

Kyries

For our disregard and neglect of your creation,
Lord have mercy
Lord have mercy.
For our indifference to the needs of others,
Christ have mercy
Christ have mercy.
For the wasting of our talents and abilities,
Lord have mercy
Lord have mercy.

Father Creator we have raped and abused your world –
Lord have mercy
Lord have mercy.
Jesus Saviour we have ignored your great love –
Christ have mercy
Christ have mercy.
Spirit, Sustainer of all, we have sought to live without
   you –
Lord have mercy
Lord have mercy.

We have failed to be good stewards of your creation –
Lord have mercy
Lord have mercy.
We have failed to be good stewards of your gospel –
Christ have mercy
Christ have mercy.
We have failed to be good stewards of your gifts –
Lord have mercy
Lord have mercy.

We have treated the world as if it were ours –
Lord have mercy
Lord have mercy.
We have treated our neighbours with little respect –
Christ have mercy
Christ have mercy.
We have treated our talents with neglect –
Lord have mercy
Lord have mercy.

Father, you have entrusted the world to our care
And we have betrayed you –
Lord have mercy
Lord have mercy.
Jesus, you have entrusted our neighbours to our care
And we have betrayed you –
Christ have mercy
Christ have mercy.
Spirit, you have entrusted your gifts into our keeping
And we have betrayed you –
Lord have mercy
Lord have mercy.

Strong deliverer, mighty God,
Have mercy upon us
Have mercy upon us.
Morning star, light of the world,
Have mercy on us
Have mercy on us.
Brooding Spirit, giver of life,
Have mercy on us
Have mercy on us.
Creator of all, Lover of all
Have mercy on us.
Redeemer of all, Saviour of all
Have mercy on us.
Guide of all, Upholder of all
Have mercy on us.

Almighty God,
who forgives all who truly repent,
have mercy upon you,
pardon and deliver you from all your sins,
confirm and strengthen you in all goodness,
and keep you in life eternal;
through Jesus Christ our Lord. Amen.

ASB

INTERCESSION

Intercession is not so much what we want from God, as discovering what He wants to do and is already doing for us. It is not that we are seeking to change God's mind, rather it is to open our minds and our lives to His action that is taking place. Too often in prayer it is not that God will not or cannot; it is that we lack vision and believe that He seems to be unwilling or unable. Often in intercession it is good to begin by opening ourselves to His grace and goodness. Affirm that God is love, and that He wants the best for His children and the whole of His creation. He offers us healing and peace, He offers us strength, He offers us Himself.

We should seek to be still like a sunbather, soaking in the love and light of the Lord. We should let His great gifts flow into our lives, open ourselves to that offering. Too often we become so uptight and full that nothing can get in. Relax, let go and let God. Know that you are enfolded, encircled by Him and His love.

Once this is done, let the ripples of this love move outward. Like throwing a stone on a pond, let it move out in ever-increasing circles.

> The Love of God flowing free
> The Love of God flow out through me.
> The Peace of God flowing free
> The Peace of God flow out through me.
> The Life of God, flowing free
> The Life of God flow out through me.[1]

Become a channel of God's grace; let God move out through you to others. As you open yourself, try to visualize it. See the goodness of God flowing through you and from you. Remember that you are only the pipeline; the gifts that flow through you are God's, but He does seek you as His channel. Visualize the person you are praying for being showered with His light, enfolded in His love, immersed in His peace. He wants those you are praying for to have these gifts; help them to flow into them.

Christ, light of the world, scatter our darkness,
Let your healing spring up with the dawn.
In the darkness around us,
Let this church be a still place of light
A still place of love
A still place of peace
A still place of your presence.
From here, Lord . . .
From this place . . .
Through us
May your light flow
May your love radiate
May your peace reach out
May your presence be known.
Make us, Lord,
A sure place of your light
A sure place of your love
A sure place of your presence.
Through us
Let your light shine
Let your love enfold
Let your peace fill
Let your presence be known.

Christ our light
Christ our might
Guard us sleeping
Let us be in your keeping
This night and evermore.

Prince of the Universe
Master of the Mysteries
Protect us in the dark hours
Until the morning light.

Christ of the wounds
Christ of the glory
Christ of the sorrows
Christ of the joys
Christ of all mysteries,
We place ourselves,
Body and soul,
Under your protection
This day and evermore.
O Christ of the outcast
O Christ of the poor
O Christ of the joyful
O Christ of the tearful,
Your presence be our protection,
Your presence be our peace,
This day and evermore.

O Christ my shield
My protector be;
O Christ my tower
My protector be;
O Christ my strength
My protector be;
O Christ my rock
My protector be;
Now and to all eternity
Now and to all eternity.

Jesus, Saviour,
Man of sorrows and acquainted with grief,
We come to you
For you alone can make us whole.

Jesus, Saviour,
Wounded for our transgressions,
Bruised for our iniquities,
We come to you
For you alone can make us whole.

Jesus, Saviour,
We come as a church broken by factions,
Weak in our mission,
Wavering in our faith.
We come to you
For you alone can make us whole.

Jesus, Saviour,
We come as people of the world,
Torn by war,
Ruined by greed,
Spoilt by selfishness.
We come to you
For you alone can make us whole.

Jesus, Saviour,
We come as members of a family,
Insensitive to each other,
Blind to tears and deaf to cries.
We come to you
For you alone can make us whole.

Jesus, Saviour,
We come with the sick at heart,
We come with the ill in mind,
We come with the diseased in body.
We come to you
For you alone can make us whole.

Jesus, you are the light of the world,
A light that no darkness can quench.

Upon your church
Wrestling with the darkness of evil,
Battling against doubt,
Let your light shine.

Upon the world governments
Facing gloom and despair,
Battling against disaster,
Let your light shine.

Upon those that live in the shadows
Caught up in sorrow and strife,
Struggling against oblivion,
Let your light shine.

Come, my Lord,
My light, my way;
Come, my lantern
Night and day;
Come, my healer,
Make me whole;
Come, my Saviour,
Protect my soul;
Come, my King,
Enter my heart;
Come, Prince of Peace,
and never depart.

We beg you, Lord, to help and defend us.
Deliver the oppressed,
Pity the insignificant,
Raise the fallen,
Show yourself to the needy,
Heal the sick,
Bring back those of your people who have
    gone astray,
Feed the hungry,
Lift up the weak,
Take off the prisoners' chains.
May every nation come to know that you are
    God alone,
That Jesus is your Son,
That we are your people, the sheep of your
    pasture.

St Clement of Rome

Holy and strong One,
In our weakness, we come to you;
Strengthen us, good Lord.
We bring a church weak in mission,
Wavering in faith,
Dwindling in numbers,
Fearful of outreach.
Strengthen us, good Lord.

We bring a world strained and stressed,
Broken by war and crime,
Discouraged by evil,
Distressed by violence.
Strengthen us, good Lord.

We bring friends in loneliness and heartache,
In weariness and want,
In fear and anxiety.
Strengthen us, good Lord.

We bring the sick and the suffering,
The pained and the despairing,
The forsaken and the betrayed.
Strengthen us, good Lord.

We bring before you, Lord,
the troubles and dangers of
peoples and nations;
the sighing of prisoners,
the sorrows of the bereaved,
the necessities of strangers,
the dependency of the weary,
the failing powers of the aged.
Lord, draw near to each
for the sake of Jesus Christ.
Augustine of Hippo (354–430)

Merciful Father,
accept these prayers
for the sake of your Son,
our Saviour Jesus Christ. Amen.
ASB

THE OFFERING

Remember, it is we who are guests at His table. We are not inviting the Lord to come among us; He has invited us to come and share with Him in the great feast of His kingdom. Whatever we bring in the way of gifts and talents it is because He has given them to us: 'All things come from you, O Lord, and of your own do we give you.' The offering is one of response, of thanksgiving for all that we have received. In the early church, the bread and wine were brought to the altar by the people to express visibly the offering of their crops, their works, themselves. So the offertory should be the whole of our lives: our joys, our sorrows, our hopes and our fears.

It is not just an offering of bread and wine, it involves all of the harvest, the sowing, reaping, transporting, milling or fermenting and all the people it takes to make the end result. It involves the climate – and the ozone layer – the sun, rain, soil and air; all this and much more is being offered. It is an offering of the whole world and it has cosmic proportions. What is involved here is the whole of creation.

Every now and again it is good at the offertory to visualize all that is to be offered. It is not just our giving for the week, it is not just money, bread and wine, it is not even the offering of our prayers and ourselves. It is something much bigger – larger than the world as we know it, embracing all of God's creation, and that will include angels and archangels and the whole company of heaven.

As we move from the offertory to the eucharistic prayer we will discover that it is not our offering alone, it is the great offering of Christ that is being offered. Because we make our offering at this point, I like sometimes to offer the intercessions along with the bread and wine. This type of prayer can be used at home over our daily food. This in turn would link our Sunday offering to our daily lives in a more definite way.

Lord of the elements, all praise to you.
Made known in the bread and wine,
Hidden God, you reveal yourself
In and through your creation.
Every creature is a sacrament.
All creation reveals your power.
Open our eyes, hidden God,
That we may see you
In your world
In all peoples
In every creature.
Let us know you love all,
That we, and all things,
Abide in you,
In your care
In your love
In your Presence
Now and evermore.

Lord,
You have gathered together your scattered peoples;
Make us one in you,
One in heart and mind,
One in thought and deed,
to serve you and do your will.

Lord, we offer ourselves to you
As we offer this bread and wine.
As the grain is gathered from the fields to make
    one loaf,
and as the grapes are gathered from the hillsides to
    make one wine,
bring us together in you.

As one family is united by their blood bonds,
Unite us in you.
As the water is mingled with the wine,
May we share in you who are Divine.
You have taken upon you our humanity,
So, Lord, may we partake in your Divinity.
As the water and wine become one
May we be one with you.

Be with us, Lord, in the breaking:
In the break of day
In the breaking of the bread
In the breaking of our lives
In the breaking of our hearts
In the breaking of our hopes.
Be with us, Lord,
For you alone can make us whole.

Be with us, Lord, in the outpouring:
In the outpouring of the wine
In the outpouring of our hopes
In the outpouring of our troubles.
Be with us, Lord, in the outpouring,
For you alone, Lord, can make us whole.

You have come among us
To be known in the breaking.
Come, Lord, come,
For you alone can make us whole.

You, Lord, are the Bread of life:
Let this bread be life giving
Let this bread be a means of growth
Let this bread be for my strengthening.
That receiving this bread,
I may be one with you.

You, Lord, are the true Vine:
Let this wine be to me for refreshment
Let this wine be to me for renewal
Let this wine be to me for joy,
That receiving this wine,
I may be one with you.

*Blessed are you, Lord God of all creation; through
your goodness we have this bread to offer, which the
earth has given and human hands have made . . .*

With this bread we rejoice in all who are
    experiencing growth and the incoming tide today.
With this bread we share with parents rejoicing in
    a new birth,
We rejoice with couples discovering a new love or
    a newness in their love,
We rejoice with employees in new work or doing
    new things at work.
Blessed be God for ever

We rejoice in all places of growth and learning,
With schools, colleges and universities,
With all church colleges and monasteries,
With all preachers and evangelists;

For all growing in stature, in wisdom and in spirit,
For infants in their classes,
For youth in their adventures,
For adults in their enthusiasm;

For those growing crops, flowers and produce,
For those working the land and caring for cattle,
For those working in industry and those at sea;
For all who will come to this place,
For all who will meet us this day,
For the freshness and the newness of this day;

We have this bread to offer, which the earth
    has given,
And human hands have made.
It will become for us the bread of life.
Blessed be God for ever.

Blessed are you, Lord God of all creation; through your goodness we have this wine to offer, which the earth has given and human hands have made . . .

We offer this wine for all who are being poured out
    and diminished this day,
For all who are experiencing the ebb tide –

For all experiencing the waning of powers,
For those losing mobility or agility,
For those whose minds can no longer cope;

We offer this wine for all families facing sickness
    or death,
For those with loved ones ill,
For all who are in hospital,
For all who are orphaned and widowed,
For all who this day will bring life on earth to a close;

For those who have been betrayed in love,
For those deceived by friends,
For those made redundant;

For those whose lives are diminished by tyranny,
For those who are belittled by oppression,
For those restricted by injustice,

For the poor of our world,
For the refugees and the homeless,
For the starving and the impoverished;

We have this wine to offer,
Made by the crushing of the grapes.
Where the Spirit ferments, it is set free,
Wine that is to be outpoured,
Fruit of the vine and work of human hands.
It will become our spiritual drink.
Blessed be God for ever.

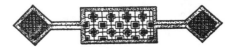

Yours, Lord, is the greatness, the power,
the glory, the splendour and the majesty;
for everything in heaven and on earth is yours.
All things come from you,
and of your own do we give you.

ASB

The Eucharistic

Prayer

At the centre of the Eucharist is the great eucharistic prayer. It is the offering of our Lord Himself to us, now in time and for all eternity. It contains the eternal relationship and love that our God always has towards us. It seeks to express deep mysteries that are beyond expression, mysteries that are there whether we are aware of them or not. This is certainly a gateway to heaven where our God comes to us and we move towards Him. Speaking of the Eucharist, St Symeon said:

I know that the immovable comes down.
I know that the invisible appears to me.
I know that He who is outside the whole creation
Takes me to Himself.

The Eucharist is not only an acting out and a remembering of the saving acts of God. It is an opportunity to share in them and to experience them more deeply for ourselves. The eucharistic prayer for that reason starts with the great affirmation, 'The Lord is here.' It is to Him we come and before Him we bow in awe and adoration. It is with such thoughts that I wrote the affirmation, 'Each Church is Bethlehem', for we are given the opportunity to be open to His coming to us. These are words on entering a church:

I open the stable door,
I kneel before the infant.
I worship with the shepherds.
I adore the Christ child.
I ponder the Word made flesh.
I absorb the love of God.
I sing glory with the angels.
I offer gifts with the magi.
I have come from lands afar.
I receive the living Lord.
I hold Him in my hands.
I go on my way rejoicing.
Glorifying and praising God.

We need to be even more open and discover we are never on our own, for each Eucharist is of the whole church. We join with angels and archangels and the whole company of heaven, with the saints, with the living and the departed. There are not many Eucharists, there is only one, and we are one together in time and through all eternity. This unity already exists in Christ and is of Christ; it is our own lack of vision that refuses to see it. When our Lord comes to us it is not simply to unite with each of us as an individual, but that we all may be one, one with Him and in Him as He is one with the Father. This oneness extends ever outwards; it is not only about all peoples but about the whole of creation; it extends to the very cosmos itself. All that exists has been and is being transformed by His consecration and we are being invited to share in it. We are indeed being faced with the deepest mysteries, and the deepest love of the whole of creation. We cannot but come in awe and adoration. Here, our hearts are to be uplifted.

What follows is not a consecration prayer but a commentary upon it, little pieces that can be added to open our awareness of some of the great actions that are taking place. I have often used this as a spoken commentary which a second person will read during the actual prayer in church.

[The Lord Jesus Christ,] in the same night that he was betrayed, took bread.[1]

> Be gentle when you touch bread.
> Let it not lie, uncared for,
> Unwanted.
> So often bread is taken for granted.
> There is such beauty in bread –
> Beauty of sun and soil,
> Beauty of patient toil.
> Wind and rain have caressed it,
> Christ often blessed it.
> Be gentle when you touch bread.
>
> *Anonymous*

[He] took bread and gave you thanks.

> Bread is a lovely thing to eat,
> God bless the barley and the wheat.
> A lovely thing to breathe is air,
> God bless the sunshine everywhere.
> The world is a lovely place to know,
> God bless the folk that come and go.
> Alive is a lovely thing to be,
> Giver of life we say Bless Thee.
>
> *Anonymous*

[He] took bread and gave you thanks; he broke it and gave it to his disciples, saying, Take, eat, this is my body which is given for you. *[Here the priest may break the bread, holding part in each hand and spreading his arms outwards to make the shape of the cross.]*

> On the holy cross I see
> Jesus' hands nailed fast for me.
> On the holy cross I see
> Jesus' feet nailed fast for me.
> Loving Jesus let me be
> Still and quiet, close to thee,
> Learning all thy love for me
> Giving all my love to thee!

[He] took bread and gave you thanks; he broke it and gave it to his disciples, saying, Take, eat; this is my body which is given for you; do this in remembrance of me.

Do this, meet together, break the bread, remember me.
Remember me at the feeding of the five thousand –
You do not have to perish in the wilderness –
Come to me, and I will refresh you,
I will renew you,
I will restore you.
Come to me, I am the bread of life,
The bread that comes down from heaven.
Remember me.
Remember me, I am known in the breaking,
In the breaking of the day and in the breaking of
    the bread.

Two people on the road to Emmaus,
Plans shattered,
Lives confused,
Hearts broken,
Knew me in the breaking.
I am there in your breaking also,
And in the breaking of the bread.

There are times when the dough is dull, soggy
    and unattractive.
Like life, at times
It has lost its sheen, the gold of the grain, the pure
    whiteness of the flour.
It looks – and it is – flat, it looks dead.
But secret things are happening,
The exciting moment is to be experienced,
The bread is rising,
The bread is rising . . . I have seen the Lord.
I have seen the Lord!

Christ has died:
Christ is risen:
Christ will come again. Alleluia.

In the same way, after supper he took the cup and gave
you thanks; he gave it to them, saying, Drink this, all of
you; this is my blood of the new covenant, which is
shed for you and for many . . .

The cup is full of blood-red wine
Made from the crushing and the bruising of
    the grapes.
By the loss of life,
By the cutting down and the pressing,
The Spirit is set free;
Allowed to ferment, the Spirit is at work.

Remember me.
Remember me, my crushing, my bruising,
My three-day fermenting,
My rising . . .
This is the wine that makes glad the hearts of all.

Christ has died:
Christ is risen:
Christ will come again. Alleluia.

Do this in remembrance of me.

Remember me.
Drink this in remembrance, all of you.
Be filled with my Spirit,
Let my life fill yours,
Inebriate you,
Give you courage,
Fill you with joy.

This is my blood of the new covenant, which is shed
for you and for many for the forgiveness of sins. Do
this, as often as you drink it, in remembrance of me.

Forgive –
As I have forgiven you,
Forgive others.
I accept you as you are –
Learn to accept others as they are.
'Love ever gives,
Forgives, outlives
And ever stands with open hands
And while it lives it gives
For this is love's prerogative
To give and give and give'.[2]

Do this in remembrance of me.

Accept through him, our great high priest,
this our sacrifice of thanks and praise;
and as we eat and drink these holy gifts
in the presence of your divine majesty,
renew us by your Spirit,
inspire us with your love,
and unite us in the body of your Son,
Jesus Christ our Lord.

ASB

THANKSGIVING

The psalmist says, 'Come into his gates with thanksgiving, enter his courts with praise.' One of the easiest ways to seek God is to think and thank; literally to count your blessings, to see the world as His creation, to see your life, and your eternal life, as in His hands. It is to take time to know that you are made by God, belong to God – in love – and will return to God.

As these realities enter into your life, the gates open and you enter into a deeper awareness of the presence and the present. With thanksgiving we need active imaging, that is, we need to stop and see what God has done for us and how wonderful is the world around us. The more we can visualize the realities of our existence the better it is for us. It is at this point that I like to think of the words of William Blake: 'If the doors of perception were cleansed, everything would appear to man as it is, infinite.'

The danger with much of life today is that it is on a very one-level plane. There is little awareness of spiritual depths or even spiritual struggles until we are in deep trouble, and then the awareness is usually negative. There are always deeper and richer worlds waiting to open up to us. Our faith should be life-expanding, helping us to fulfil ourselves and to enjoy our God-given world. Here the prayers of thanksgiving play an important part, for they open us up and help us to appreciate what is around us. To say grace at meals can be a good start for many. Even here we need to realize that we are not inviting God but that He has invited and provided for us; as they say on the island of Lewis, 'We are God's guests and 'tis He who keeps a generous table.'

I often offer the idea of prayers of thanksgiving to the sad and the down in spirit, for here again thanksgiving opens up a new vista. It is very hard to have a sad heart and be thankful at the same time. The cure for our heaviness is to rejoice in the Lord and all He has done and is doing for us. The more we appreciate things, the more we learn to care for them. We learn also that these 'things' have long cared for us and our world. Thanksgiving therefore has a place in the concern for the ecological state of our planet. If we are truly grateful for the air we breathe and the water we drink, we will respect them, and certainly avoid polluting them; we will learn to care for them as they have for us. If we are grateful for the diversity of nature, we will rejoice in works of conservation and protection.

Such thanksgiving leads us naturally into sharing in the redeeming of our world – not only thanks *giving* but thanks *living* – our appreciation of our wonderful and mysterious world being reflected in our actions, our awareness of our good and gracious God, seen in the way we are generous and giving also. It is also being more aware of the great unity of all of creation. Thanksgiving has an important place in the stewardship of our whole cosmos. Thanksgiving literally has the power to transform our world.

Thanks be to thee, O God,
That I have risen today.
I have risen to life,
I have risen to love.
Thanks be to thee, O God.
You have opened my eyes,
You have given me breath,
You have made me move.
Thanks be to thee, O God,
For you walk with me,
For I dwell in you,
And you dwell in me.
Thanks be to thee, O God,
For this day and my rising.

God of the elements, glory to you.
Glory to you for flowing air
Glory for light beyond compare
Glory for water as it flows
Glory for soil and all that grows
Glory for life and love and birth
Glory to you, Lord of the earth.

Teach your children
what we have taught our children –
that the earth is our mother.
Whatever befalls the earth
befalls the sons and daughters of the earth.
If men spit upon the ground
they spit upon themselves.

This we know
The earth does not belong to us,
we belong to the earth.
This we know
All things are connected
Like the blood which unites one family.
All things are connected.

Whatever befalls the earth
befalls the sons and daughters of the earth.
We did not weave the web of life,
we are merely a strand in it.
Whatever we do to the web,
we do to ourselves.

Chief Seattle[1]

Lord, you have invited us
To be guests at your table.
You have welcomed us
Into your Presence.
You have fed us
with your body.
You have refreshed us.
With your blood
You have given us of your own self.
Help us to give ourselves to you,
In joy and thanksgiving,
In love and dedication.
As you give us freely,
Let us give freely to you.

Grant, O Lord Jesus,
That the hands which have held you
May be used to your glory.
That the lips which have taken of you
May sing your praises.
That the body which contains you
May be full of your life.
Lord, you have received us in love
And given us of yourself,
Help us to receive you with joy
And give ourselves to you.

Lord, our minds seek to know you,
Our hearts long to find you,
Our souls desire to serve you.
Send us out, aware of your Presence,
That our hearts may be renewed,
Our minds refreshed,
Our souls restored,
That we may reveal you to others,
And know you ourselves,
As Jesus Christ our Lord.

Praise be to you, Lord Jesus Christ;
You were rich, but for our sakes became poor
So that through your poverty our lives may
    be enriched.
You were strong, but for our sakes became weak
So that through your weakness we may be made
    strong.
You were light, but for our sakes entered darkness
So that through the darkness you bring us to
    light everlasting.
You were life, but for our sakes accepted death
So that through your death we may have
    life eternal.

Lord, in this blessed sacrament
You give us life
You give us love
You give us yourself.
You come to us
Dwell with us
Abide with us.
There is nothing more we can ask.

Let us give ourselves to you
Our minds
Our bodies
Our hearts
Our wills
All that we are, all that we hope to be.
Accept what we are
Consecrate us
Bless us
Transform us
That we may also reveal your presence
And be a sign of your saving love,
That we may live to your glory
And the bringing in of your kingdom.

Thanks be to thee, my Lord Jesus Christ,
For all the benefits thou hast won for me,
For all the pains and insults thou hast borne for me.
O most merciful Redeemer, Friend and Brother,
May I know thee more clearly,
Love thee more dearly,
And follow thee more nearly,
Day by day.

Richard of Chichester (1197–1253)

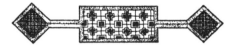

Father of all, we give you thanks and praise, that
when we were still far off you met us in your Son
and brought us home. Dying and living,
he declared your love, gave us grace,
and opened the gate of glory.
May we who share Christ's body live his risen life;
we who drink his cup bring life to others;
we whom the Spirit lights give light to the world.
Keep us firm in the hope you have set before us,
so we and all your children shall be free,
and the whole earth live to praise your name;
through Christ our Lord. Amen.

ASB

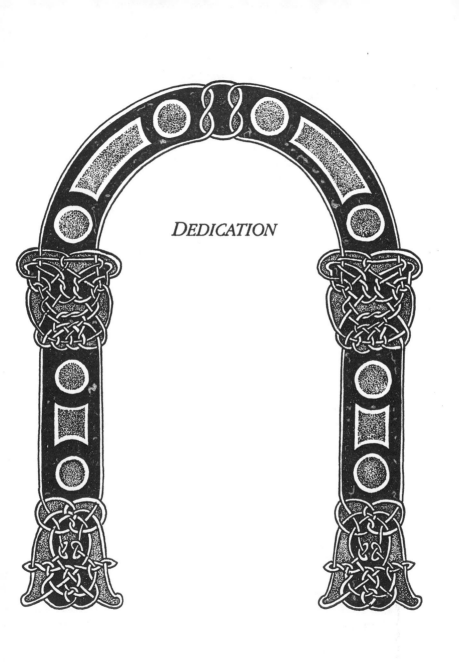

DEDICATION

Not only is God forever giving us gifts, He is giving us Himself. In fact it is because He gives us Himself, that His gifts are available to us. God is present in our lives and the more we open ourselves to Him, the more His gifts are able to flow into us and through us. The more open we become to God, the more open we become to other people and to all of His creation. Dedicating ourselves to God is a response to His giving Himself to us. It is also a promise to deal with His world and all that is in it in a particular way: 'Your will be done on earth as it is in heaven.' It is a call to adventure and to be pilgrims for the love of God, to be open to His call and His challenge.

Openness is the opposite of being dammed, or blocked. We have to stop being dammed people! We have to become far more open in our dealings. In dedicating ourselves to His service, we are offering to be channels of His gifts. This is an exciting road to take, of which there should be no ending.

One of the tragedies of today is the lack of dedication. People are almost afraid to give themselves to each other, afraid to throw themselves into a cause that will make any demands of them. Yet to give ourselves is not to empty ourselves but to be fulfilled, to learn that 'it is in giving that we receive'. A bit of advice from a social reformer of the last century was, 'Give yourself to a good cause, you may not do much for it but it will transform you.'

Again and again I have learnt that it is when I go out to give of myself, my time and my money, that I am enriched. So often the person who was to be the receiver is the person who has given new wealth to me. If we keep ourselves to ourselves we are impoverished. If we give ourselves to each other and to our God, we are enriched indeed.

I give myself to you, Lord,
I give myself to you.
All that I am
All that I have been
All that I hope to be,
I give myself to you, Lord.
I give myself to you,
In joy and in sorrow
In sickness and in health
In success and in failure,
I give myself to you, Lord,
I give myself to you.
In darkness and in light
In trouble and in joy
In time and for eternity,
I give myself to you, Lord,
I give myself to you.

Father,
In the awareness of your presence,
Beneath the shadow of your wings,
In the closeness of your love,
                    May we abide.

Jesus,
In the fellowship of your saints,
In the communion of the faithful,
In the church called to mission,
                    May we abide.

Spirit,
In the power of your love,
In the fullness of your gifts,
In the guidance of your wisdom,
                    May we abide.

God to enfold me,
God to surround me,
God in my speaking,
God in my thinking.

God in my sleeping,
God in my waking,
God in my watching,
God in my hoping.

God in my life,
God in my lips,
God in my soul,
God in my heart.

God in my sufficing,
God in my slumber,
God in my ever-living soul,
God in mine eternity.

Carmina Gadelica[1]

Teach us, good Lord, to serve thee as Thou deservest,
To give and not to count the cost,
To fight and not to heed the wounds,
To toil and not to seek for rest,
To labour and not to ask for any reward,
Save that of knowing that we do thy will.

Ignatius Loyola (1491–1556)

Lord make me an instrument of your peace.
Where there is hatred, let me sow love,
Where there is injury, pardon,
Where there is doubt, faith,
Where there is despair, hope,
Where there is darkness, light,
Where there is sadness, joy.

O Divine Master, grant that I may not so much seek
To be consoled as to console,
To be understood as to understand,
To be loved as to love;
For it is in giving that we receive,
It is in pardoning that we are pardoned,
It is in dying that we are born to eternal life.

Attributed to St Francis of Assisi (1181–1226)

God be in my head,
and in my understanding;
God be in my eyes,
and in my looking;
God be in my mouth,
and in my speaking;
God be in my heart,
and in my thinking;
God be at my end,
and at my departing.

Sarum Book of Hours (1514)

We commend unto thee, O Lord,
our souls and bodies,
our minds and our thoughts,
our prayers and our hopes,
our health and our work,
our life and our death,
our parents and brothers and sisters,
our benefactors and our friends,
our neighbours and our countrymen,
and all Christian folk,
this day and always.

Lancelot Andrewes (1555–1626)

Lord, you have welcomed us,
You have healed us
You have restored us
You have fed us
You have empowered us.
Send us out
to live and work to your glory.
Send us out
to reveal your Presence.
Send us out
to declare your love.
Send us out
To proclaim your goodness.
This day and always.

Lord, you draw near to us,
Let us draw near to you.
You are present in this Sacrament,
Abide with us always.
Abide with us in our daily lives
Abide with us in our work
Abide with us when we rest
Abide with us in our journeying
Abide with us in our homes
Abide with us at all times
And through eternity.

Grant, O Lord, that we may
Live in thy fear,
Die in thy favour,
Rest in thy peace,
Rise in thy power,
Reign in thy glory;
For thine own beloved Son's sake,
Jesus Christ our Lord.
William Laud (1573–1645)

Strengthen, O Lord, the hands that holy things
have taken, that they may daily bring forth
fruit to thy glory.
Grant, O Lord, that the lips which have sung thy
praises within the sanctuary may glorify
thee for ever;
That the ears which have heard the voice of thy
songs may be closed to the voice of
clamour and dispute;
That the eyes which have seen thy great love,
may also behold thy blessed hope.
That the tongues which have sung the *sanctus*
may ever speak the truth;
Grant that the feet that have trodden thy holy
courts may ever walk in the light;
That the souls and bodies, which have tasted of thy
living body and blood, may ever be restored
to newness of life.

Liturgy of Malabar

O Love, I give myself to Thee, Thine ever, only
  Thine to be.
This day I consecrate all that I have or hope to be
  to Thy service.
O crucified Lord, forgive the sins of my past life;
  fold me in the embrace of Thy all-prevailing
  sacrifice; purify me by the passion.
Son of man, hallow all my emotions and affections,
  and make them strong only for Thy service.
Eternal word, sanctify my thoughts;
  make them free with the freedom of Thy Spirit.
Son of God, consecrate my will to Thyself;
  unite it with Thine.
King of glory, my Lord and Master, take my whole
  being:
  use it in Thy service, and draw it ever closer to
  Thyself.

Cosmo Gordon Lang (1864–1945)

Christ of the seven directions is with me.
Christ above me to uplift me
Christ beneath me to support me
Christ before me to guide me
Christ behind me to protect me
Christ on my left to meet me
Christ on my right to greet me
Christ within me to strengthen me.

I give myself as I face east
And to the rising of the sun.
I give myself as I face south
And the fullness of this day.
I give myself as I face west
And the evening of my life.
I give myself as I face north
And the darkness before me.
I look up to the God above me,
I look down to the everlasting arms.
I have hope, for God is within me,
This day and for ever more,
This day and for ever more.

Thou who art over us,
Thou who art one of us,
Thou who *art* –
Also within us,
May all see Thee – in me also,
May I prepare the way for Thee,
May I thank Thee for all that shall fall to my lot,
May I also not forget the need of others.
Keep me in Thy love
As Thou wouldest that all should be kept in mine.
May everything in my being be directed to Thy glory
And may I never despair,
For I am under Thy hand,
And in Thee is all power and goodness.

Dag Hammarskjöld (1905–1961)[2]

Almighty God,
we thank you for feeding us
with the body and blood of your Son Jesus Christ.
Through him we offer you our souls and bodies
to be a living sacrifice.
Send us out
in the power of your Spirit
to live and work to your praise and glory. Amen.

ASB

Blessings

Blessings are what God bestows upon us, continually. His whole action towards us is blessing, from the blessing of life itself to the gifts He showers upon us. The great blessings are the gift of Himself, and the gift of eternal life. No blessing is ours by right, but in His love He offers them to us all freely. Grace is the free action of God to us. What we are asked to do is to respond, to allow the blessing to work, and to see God at work in our lives.

Blessings must not be confined to a service; these are only expressions of the reality. Blessings are to be discovered, voiced and lived in our day-to-day life. Blessings are not the domain of the priest even though liturgical blessings are kept for the priest. Blessings are what a mother bestows upon her family, what a worker bestows on his firm, what a good citizen bestows upon her community. And all these blessings are gifts from God to us and working through us. I believe it is good to carry blessings around with us. Even if we cannot say them out loud we can express them, visualize them and try to live them. It was with this in mind that I wrote this prayer.

Lord,
Make me a blessing.
Those that I meet
Make me a blessing.
As I walk down the street
Make me a blessing.
This day, even this hour
Make me a blessing.
It lies in your power
Make me a blessing.
At work and at home
Make me a blessing.
Wherever I roam
Make me a blessing.

That people may see
I am a blessing,
For you are with me.

Here, God is the subject and active, it is His blessing and we are the instrument. I have discovered very often that, if I have sought to give a blessing – even non-verbal – I have received a blessing in turn. In seeking to share blessings we discover that they are not a one-way process: the giver often receives, the God whom we seek to bring meets us there; the person we sought to help is often a great help to us. Blessings are yet another open gate and the traffic as always is two-way flowing, from us to others and from others to us. The traffic is also between heaven and earth, and earth and heaven. The gate is open, the entering is part of our pilgrimage and the invitation to life in all its fullness.

Some of the blessings that follow could be used at the Peace in the communion service as well as at the end. Both the Peace and blessings are something we need to share with others all the time. Little 'Peace be with you' prayers spoken aloud or thought during the day will help us to know that our God, His peace, and His blessings are open to us.

Pray for peace
Speak of peace
Think of peace
Act in peace,
And the peace of the Lord
be always with you.

The Creator who brought order out of chaos,
give peace to you.
The Saviour who stilled the raging storm,
give peace to you.
The Spirit who broods on the deeps,
give peace to you.

God grant you peace,
to achieve peace
to radiate peace
to extend peace
to live in peace.

The Lord who conquered darkness with light,
give peace to you.
The Lord who conquered death with life,
give peace to you.
The Lord who conquered loneliness with love,
give peace to you.

God show you the way of peace
that you may receive peace,
that you may give peace,
that you may live peace,
that you may share peace,
that the peace of God shine in you.
God be with you to guide you,
God be with you to protect you,
God be with you to strengthen you.
God be above you to uplift you,
God be beneath you to support you.
And the blessing of God Almighty,
the Father, the Son and the Holy Spirit,
Be with you, and remain with you,
Now and always.

In the full tide of the day and in its ebbing,
In the rising of the sun and its setting,
The mighty God be with you
The loving God protect you
The holy God guide you.
And the blessing . . .

Throughout the day, the good God encompass you;
Throughout the night, the saving God enfold you;
Throughout your life, the loving God behold you.
And the blessing . . .

The Father of many resting places grant you rest;
The Christ who stilled the storm grant you calm;
The Spirit who fills all things grant you peace.
God's light be your light,
God's love be your love,
God's way be your way.
And the blessing . . .

God of the heights protect and uplift you;
Christ of the depths uphold and sustain you;
Spirit of the slopes guide you and grasp you.

The arm of God be about you,
The way of Christ guide you,
The strength of the Spirit support you.

God be with you on the smooth paths;
Christ be with you in the storms;
The Spirit be with you at all times.

The holy God encircle you and keep you safe;
The mighty God defend you from all dangers;
The loving God give you his peace.

As Thou wast before
At my life's beginning,
Be Thou so again
  At my journey's end.

As Thou wast besides
At my soul's shaping,
Father be Thou too
  At my journey's close.
Carmina Gadelica[1]

Deep peace, pure white of the moon to you.
Deep peace, pure green of the grass to you.
Deep peace, pure brown of the earth to you.
Deep peace, pure grey of the dew to you.
Deep peace, pure blue of the sky to you.
Deep peace of the running wave to you.
Deep peace of the flowing air to you.
Deep peace of the quiet earth to you.
Deep peace of the shining stars to you.
Deep peace of the Son of Peace to you.
Fiona Macleod (1855–1905)

To God the Father, who first loved us,
and made us accepted in the Beloved;
To God the Son, who loved us,
and washed us from our sins in his own blood;
To God the Holy Ghost, who sheds the love of God
abroad in our hearts,
Be all love and all glory
For time and for eternity

Thomas Ken (1637–1711)

Be the peace of the Spirit mine this night,
Be the peace of the Son mine this night,
Be the peace of the Father mine this night,
The peace of all peace be mine this night,
Each morning and evening of my life.

Carmina Gadelica[2]

I am beseeching Thee
To keep me from ill,
To keep me from hurt,
To keep me from harm;

To keep me from mischance,
To keep me from grief,
To keep me this night
   In the nearness of Thy love.

May God shield me,
May God fill me,
May God keep me,
May God watch me.

Carmina Gadelica[3]

May God bring me
  To the land of peace,
  To the country of the King,
    To the peace of the eternity.

  Praise to the Father,
  Praise to the Son,
  Praise to the Spirit,
    The Three in One.
                    Carmina Gadelica[4]

The peace of God, which passes all understanding,
        keep your hearts and minds
    in the knowledge and love of God, and
      of his Son Jesus Christ our Lord;
      and the blessing of God almighty,
    the Father, the Son, and the Holy Spirit,
be among you, and remain with you always. Amen.
                    ASB

    Christ the Gateway and the Door
      give us life for evermore.

NOTES

INTRODUCTION
1 Robert Browning, 'Bishop Blougram's Apology', from *Men and Women* (1855).
2 Frances Hodgson Burnett, *The Secret Garden* (1911).

PREPARATION
1 Levi Yitzchak of Beritchev, from *Another Day – Prayers of the Human Family* (Triangle 1986), page 48.
2 In each case, the ascription *ASB* refers to *The Alternative Service Book 1980*, copyright © Central Board of Finance of the Church of England.

CANDLE PRAYERS
1 *The Promise of His Glory* (Mowbray/Cassell 1991), page 11.
2 *Prymer*, a manual of prayer for private use published in 1559.
3 Alexander Carmichael (ed.), *Carmina Gadelica* (Scottish Academic Press, reprint 1983), Volume 1, page 231.
4 Kontakion (hymn) from the Eastern Orthodox Church, from *A Manual of Eastern Orthodox Prayers* (SPCK 1945), page 23.

ADORATION
1 Teilhard de Chardin, *Le Milieu Divin* (Collins Fontana 1975), page 127.
2 Alistair MacLean, *Hebridean Altars* (Edinburgh 1937), pages 40–41.
3 *Carmina Gadelica*, Volume 1, page 3.
4 *Carmina Gadelica*, Volume 3, page 4.
5 Joseph P. Clancy, *The Earliest Welsh Poetry* (Macmillan 1970).
6 *Praying With Saint Francis* (Triangle 1987), page 16–17.

CONFESSION
1 Evelyn Underhill, from *Heaven A Dance: An Evelyn Underhill Anthology*, edited by Stuart and Brenda Blanch (Triangle 1992).

INTERCESSION

1 David Adam, *Tides and Seasons* (Triangle 1989), page 51.

THE EUCHARISTIC PRAYER

1 Text in bold in this chapter is from *The Alternative Service Book 1980.*
2 'Love ever gives . . .' by John Oxenham, *Bees In Amber.*

THANKSGIVING

1 Chief Seattle of the Du Warnish League delivered the speech from which these words are taken to the President of the United States in Washington in 1854.

DEDICATIONS

1 *Carmina Gadelica*, Volume 3, page 53.
2 Dag Hammarskjöld, *Markings* (Faber 1964), page 95.

BLESSINGS

1 *Carmina Gadelica*, Volume 3, pages 65–6.
2 *Carmina Gadelica*, Volume 3, page 337.
3 *Carmina Gadelica*, Volume 3, page 45.
4 *Carmina Gadelica*, Volume 3, page 47.